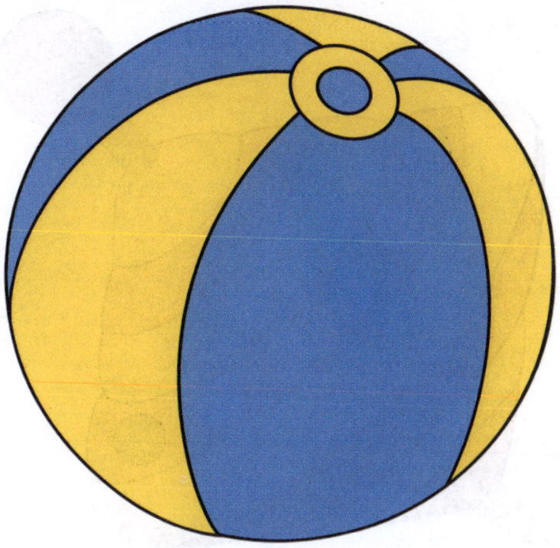

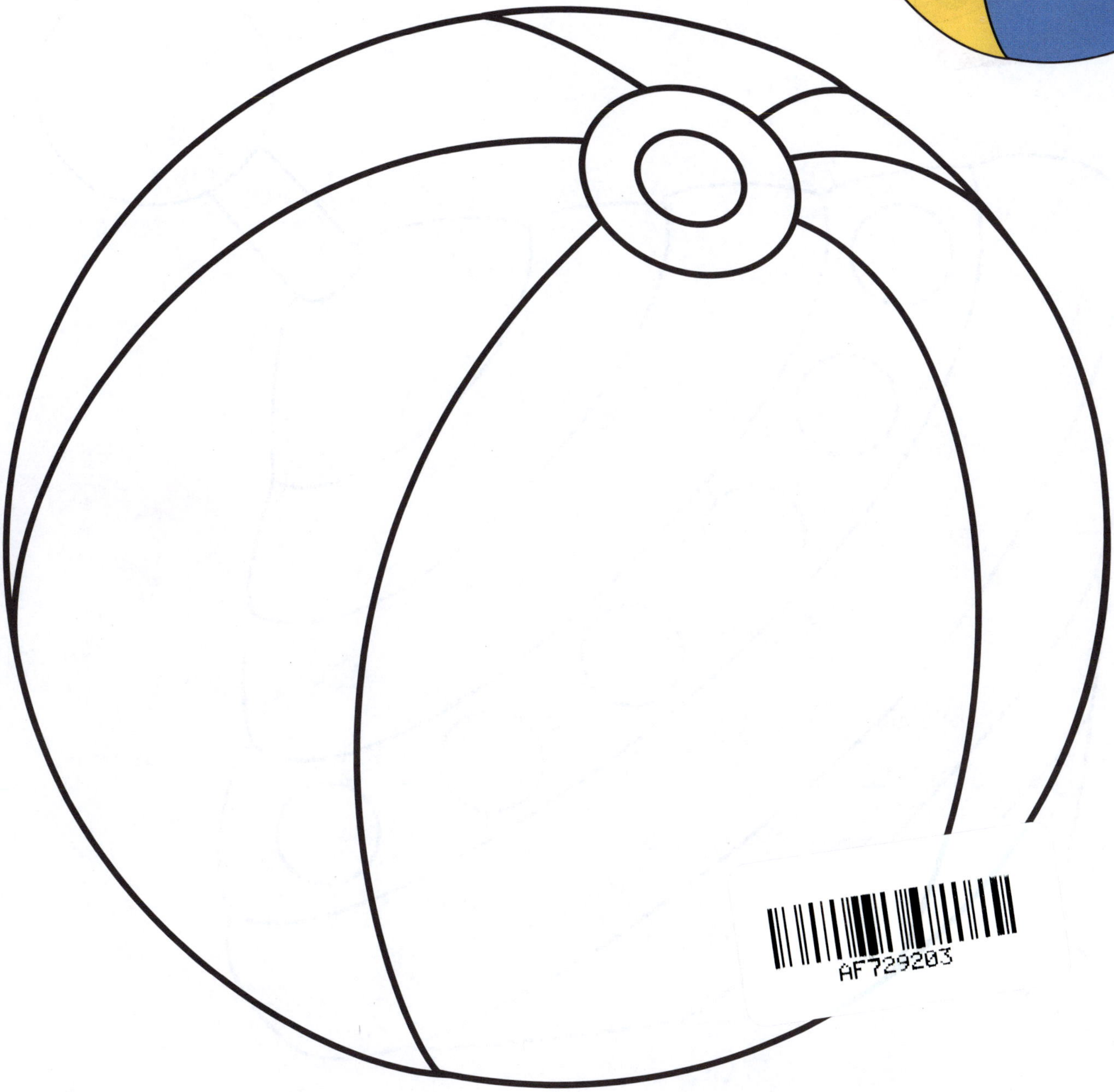

ball

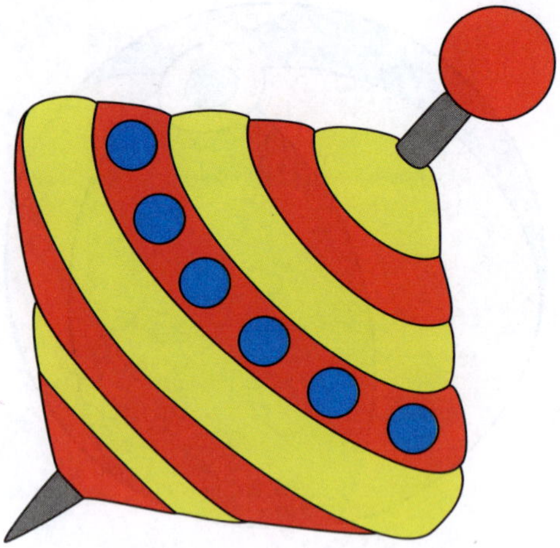

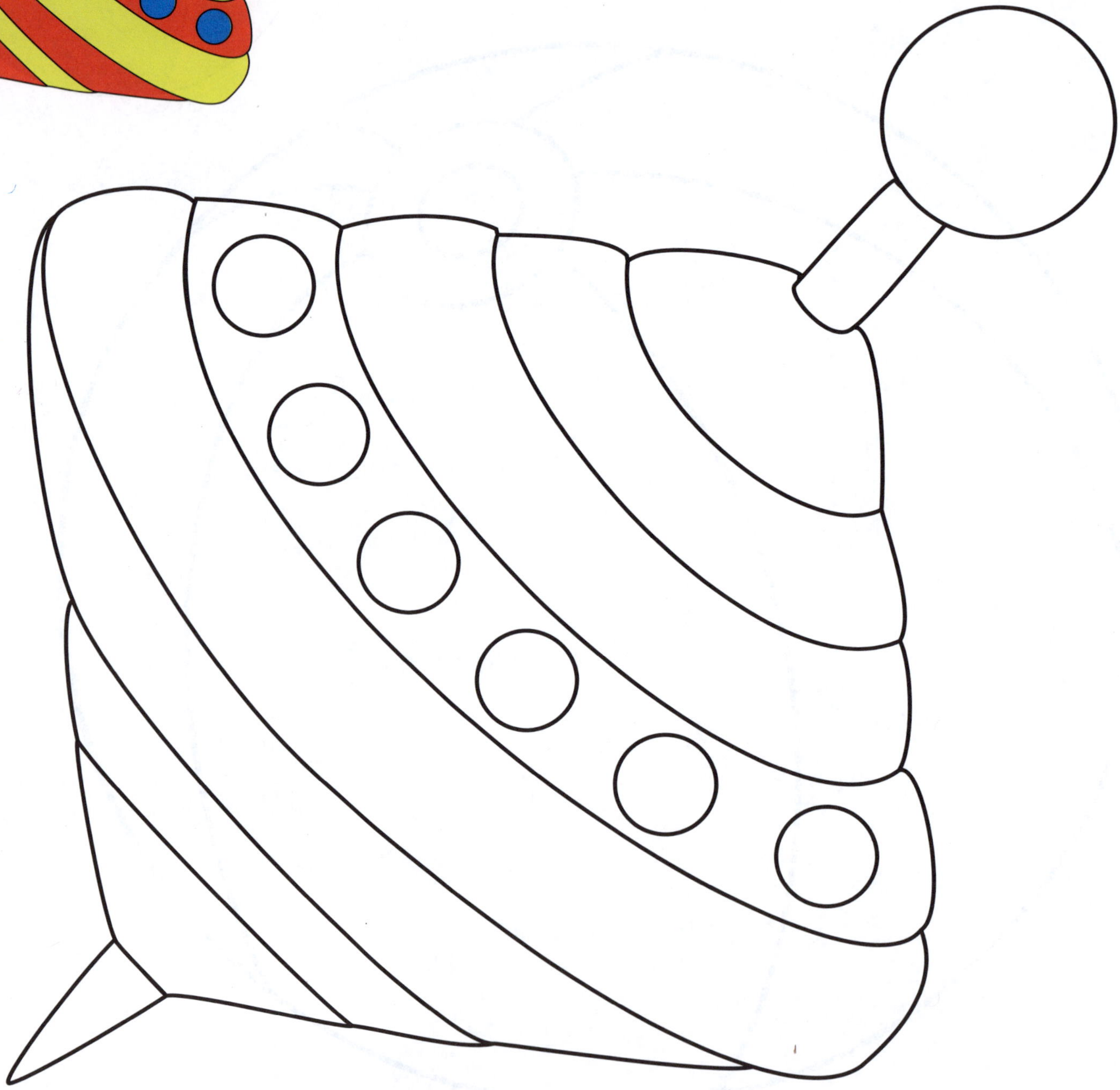

top

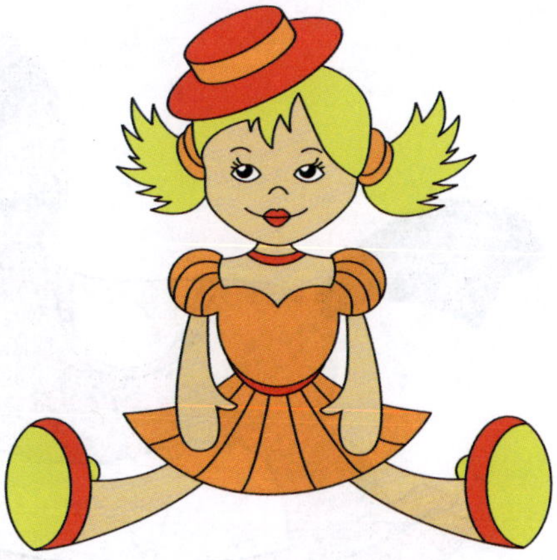

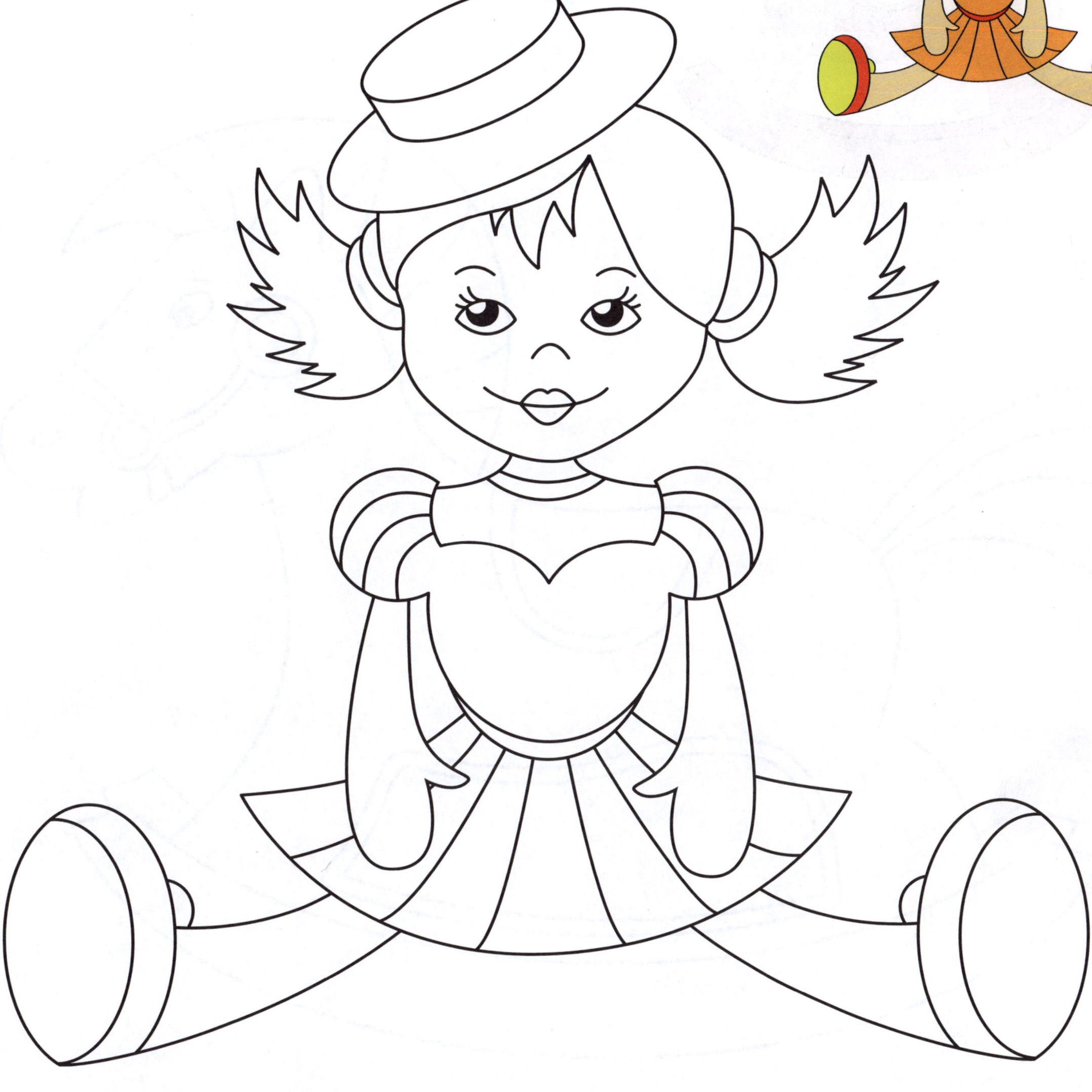

doll

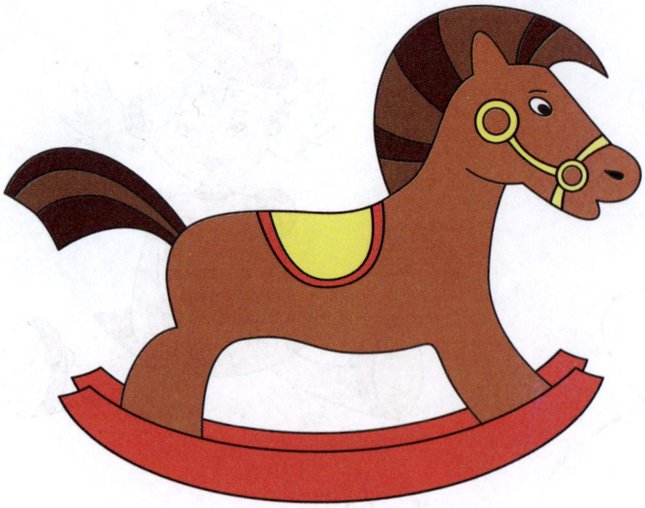

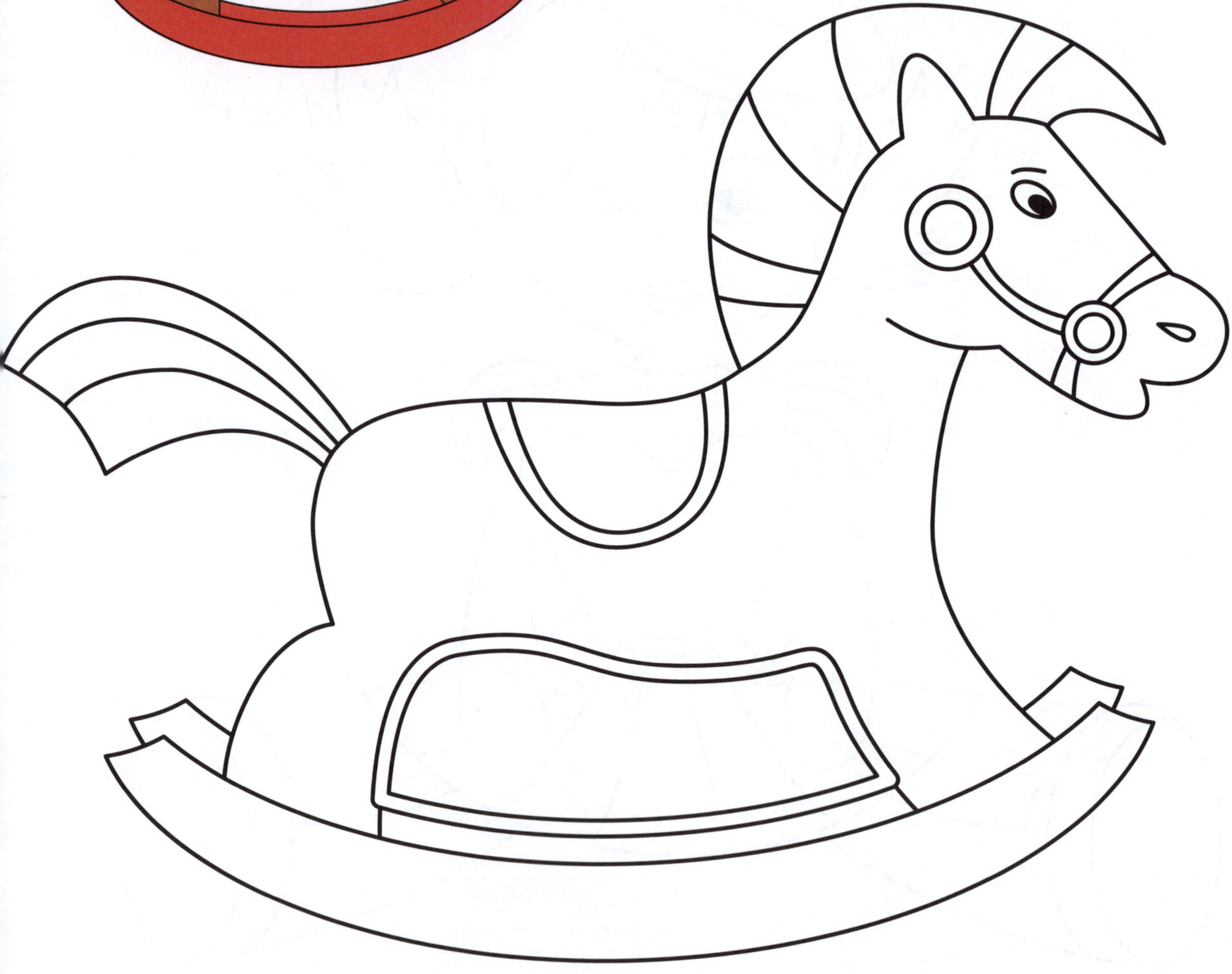

rocking horse

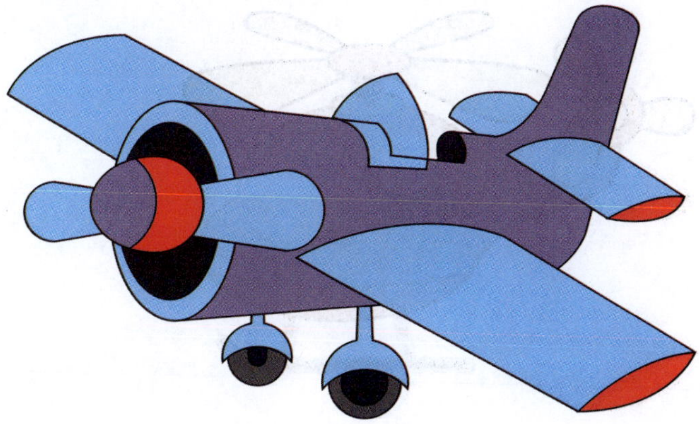

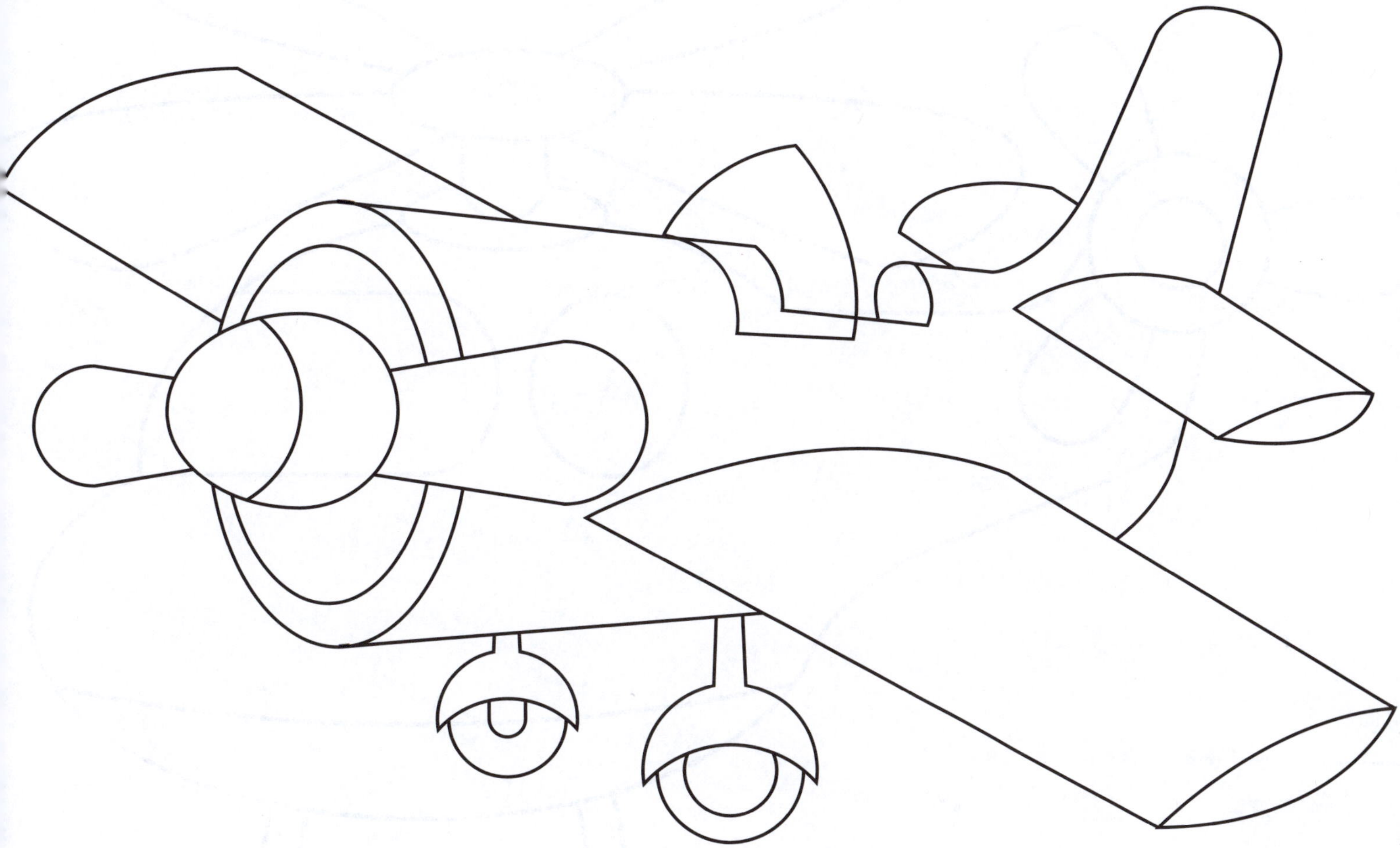

aircraft

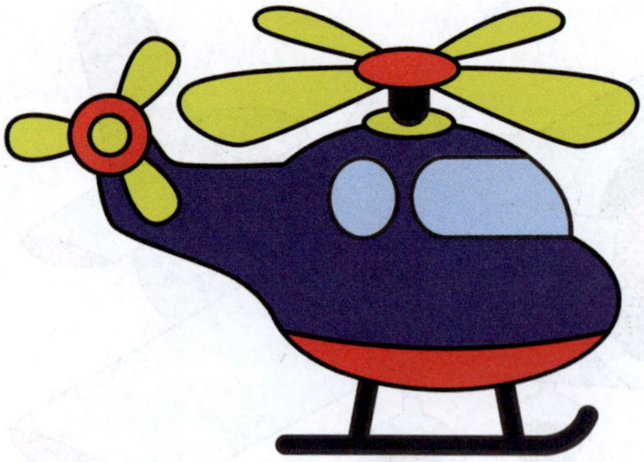

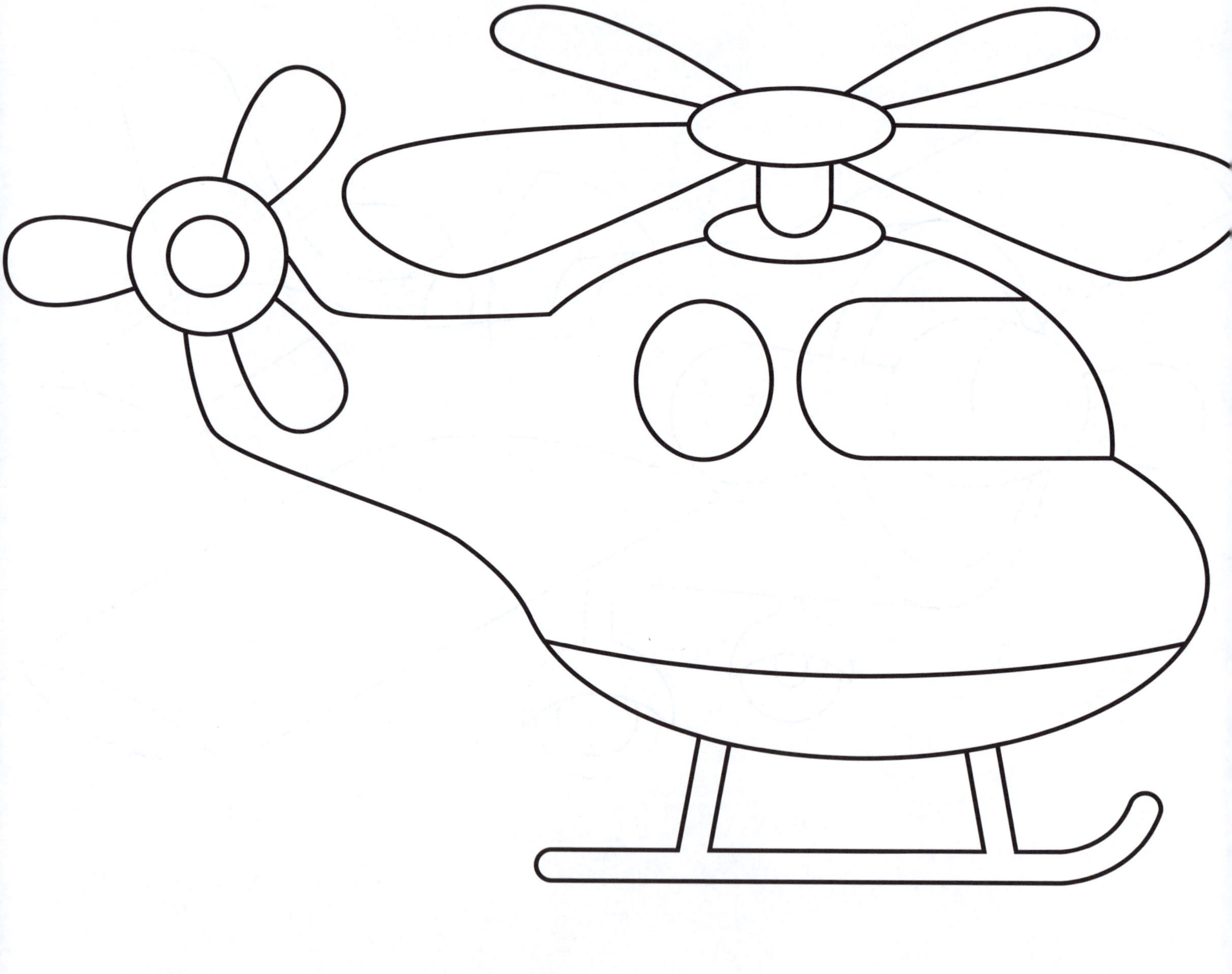

helicopter

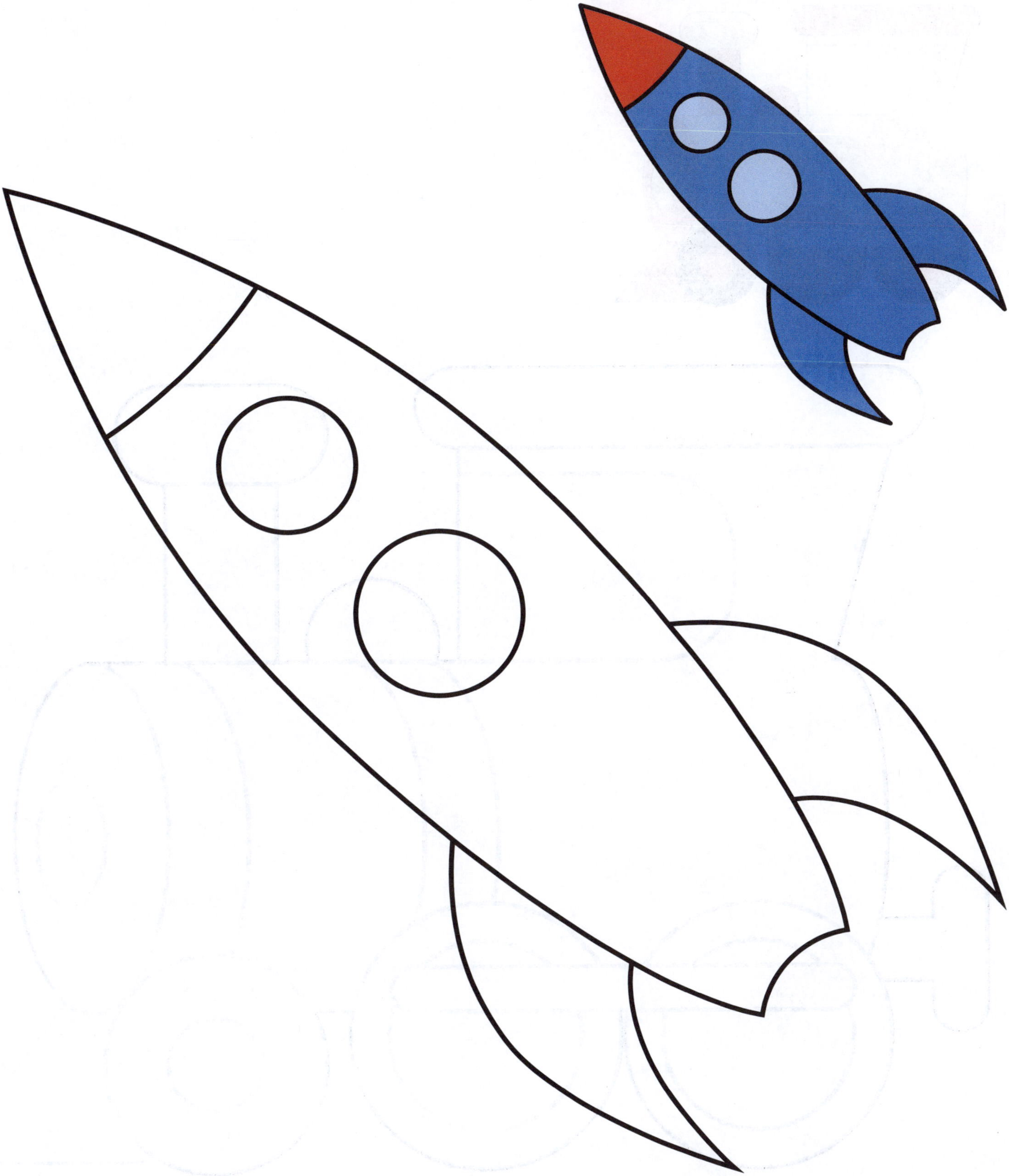

rocket

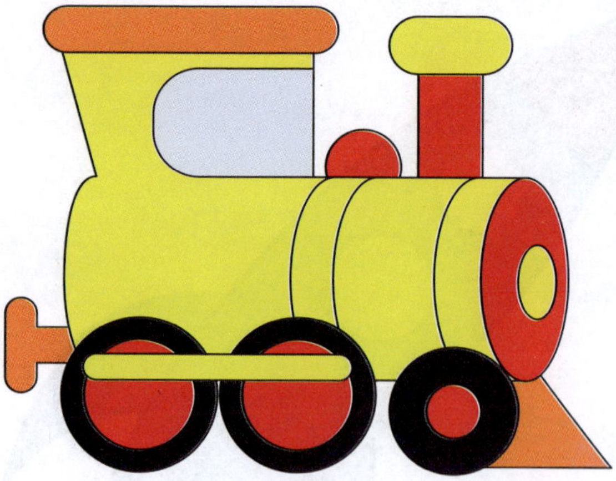

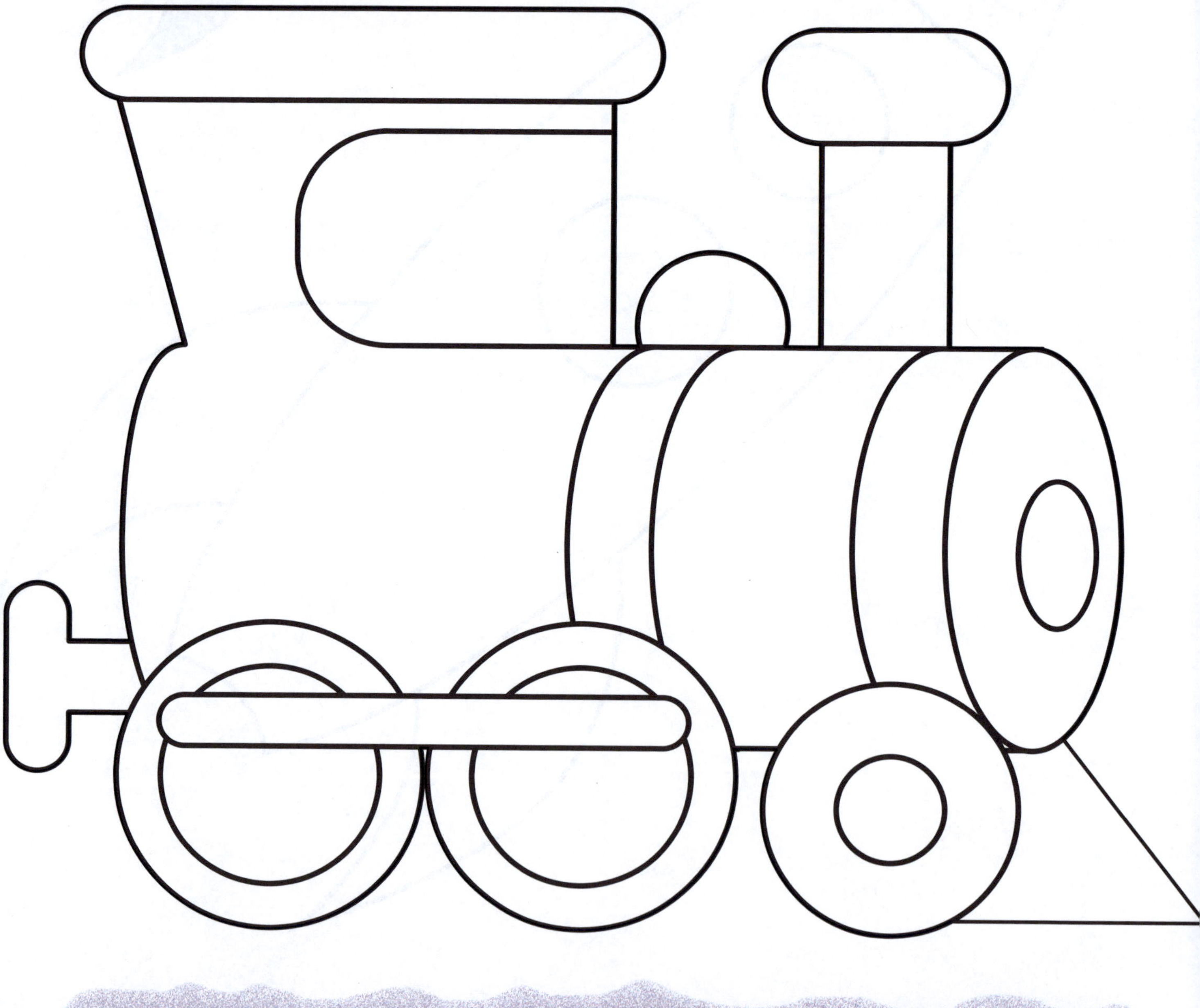

engine

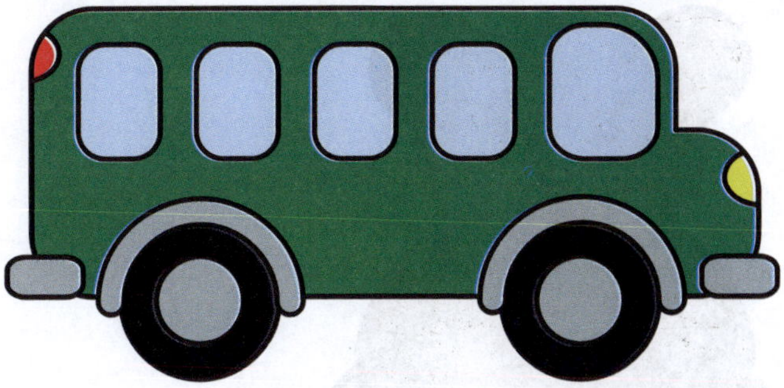

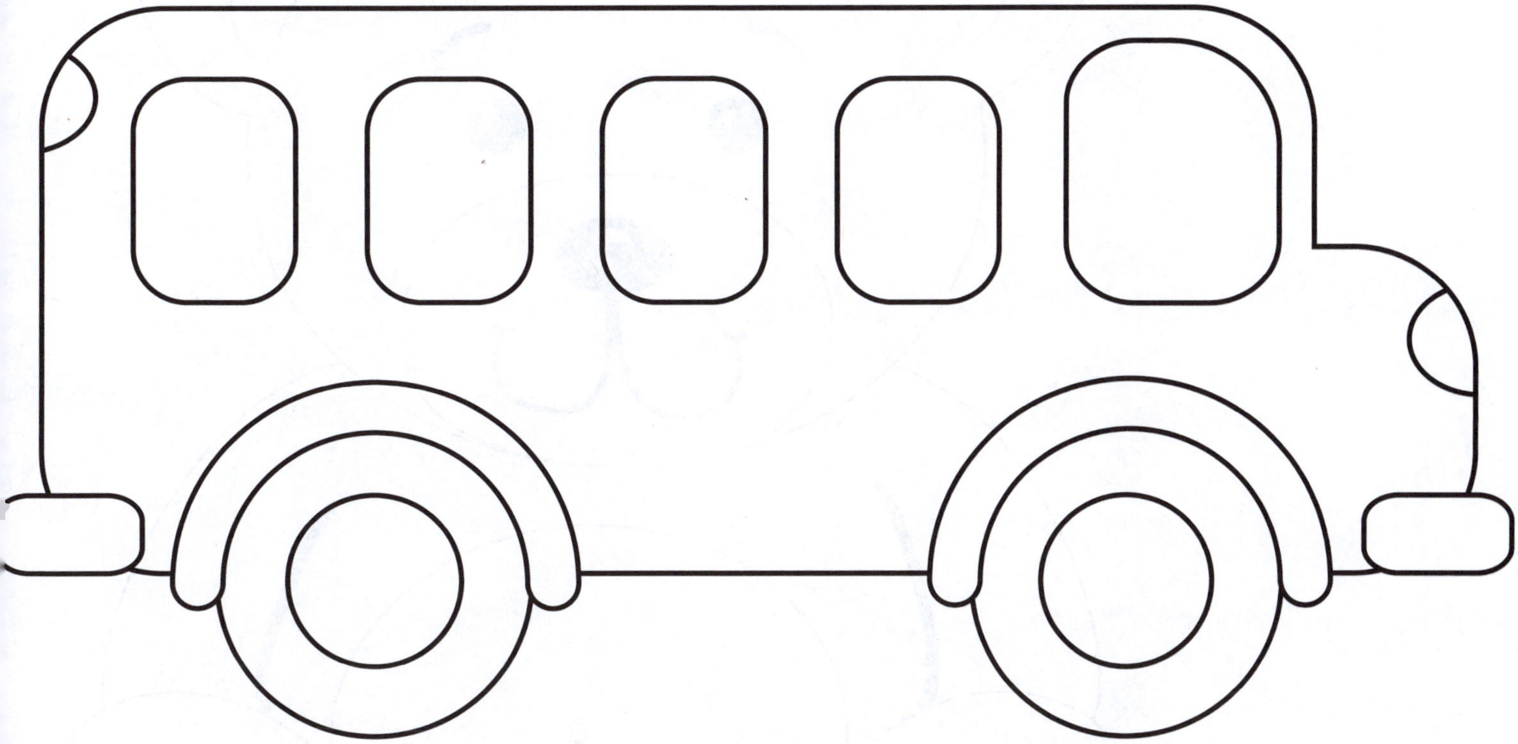

bus

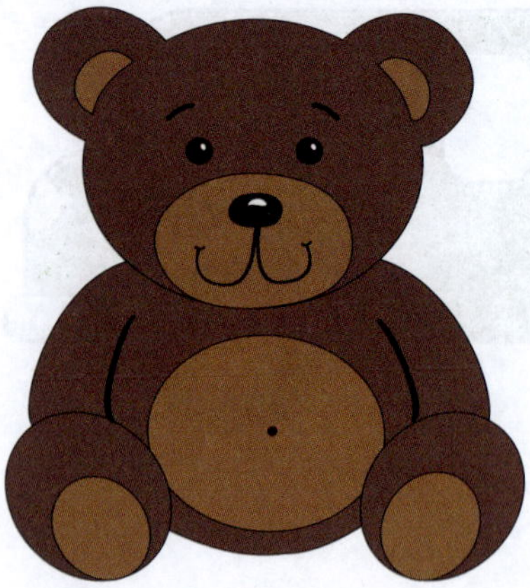

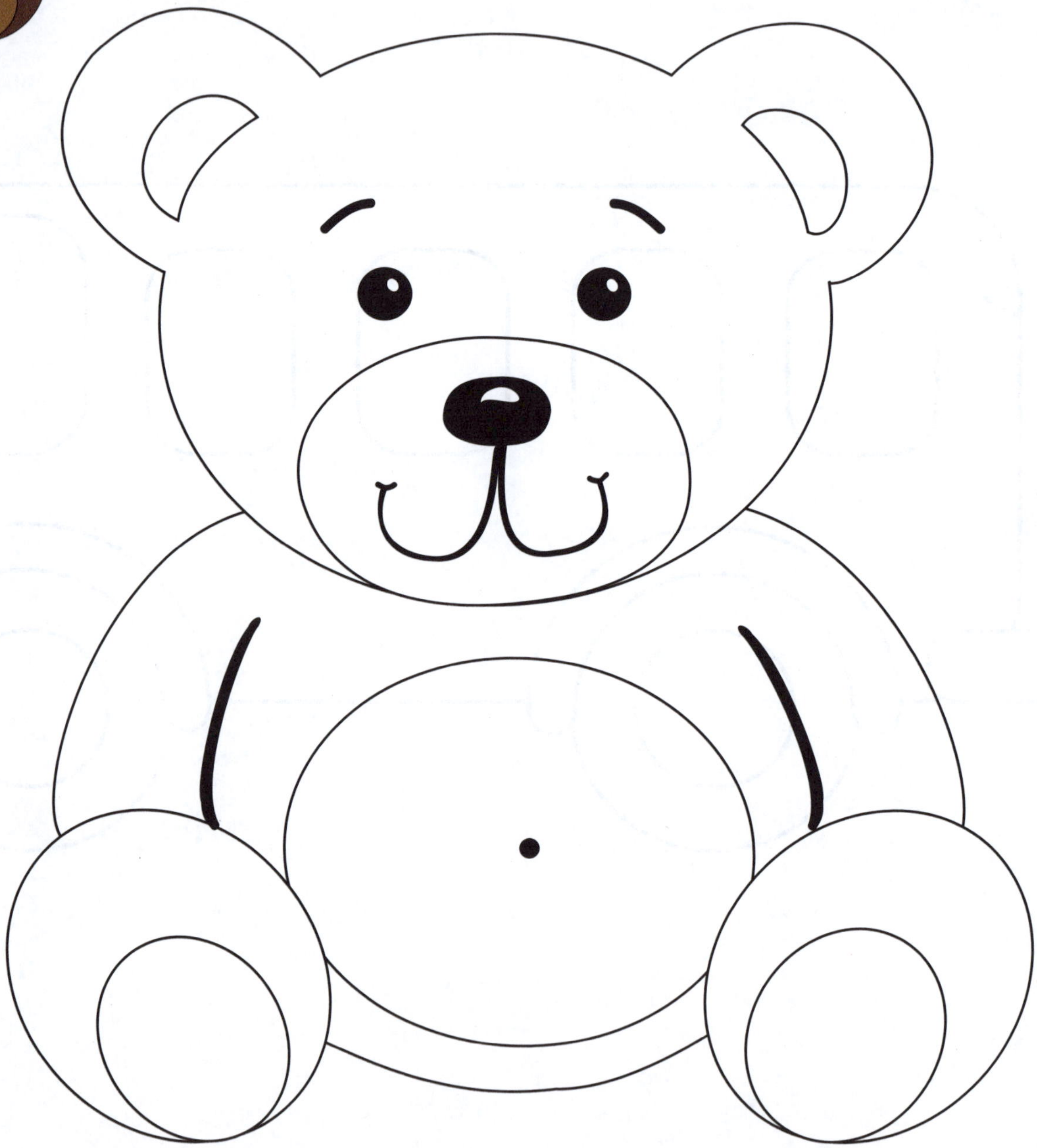

teddy bear

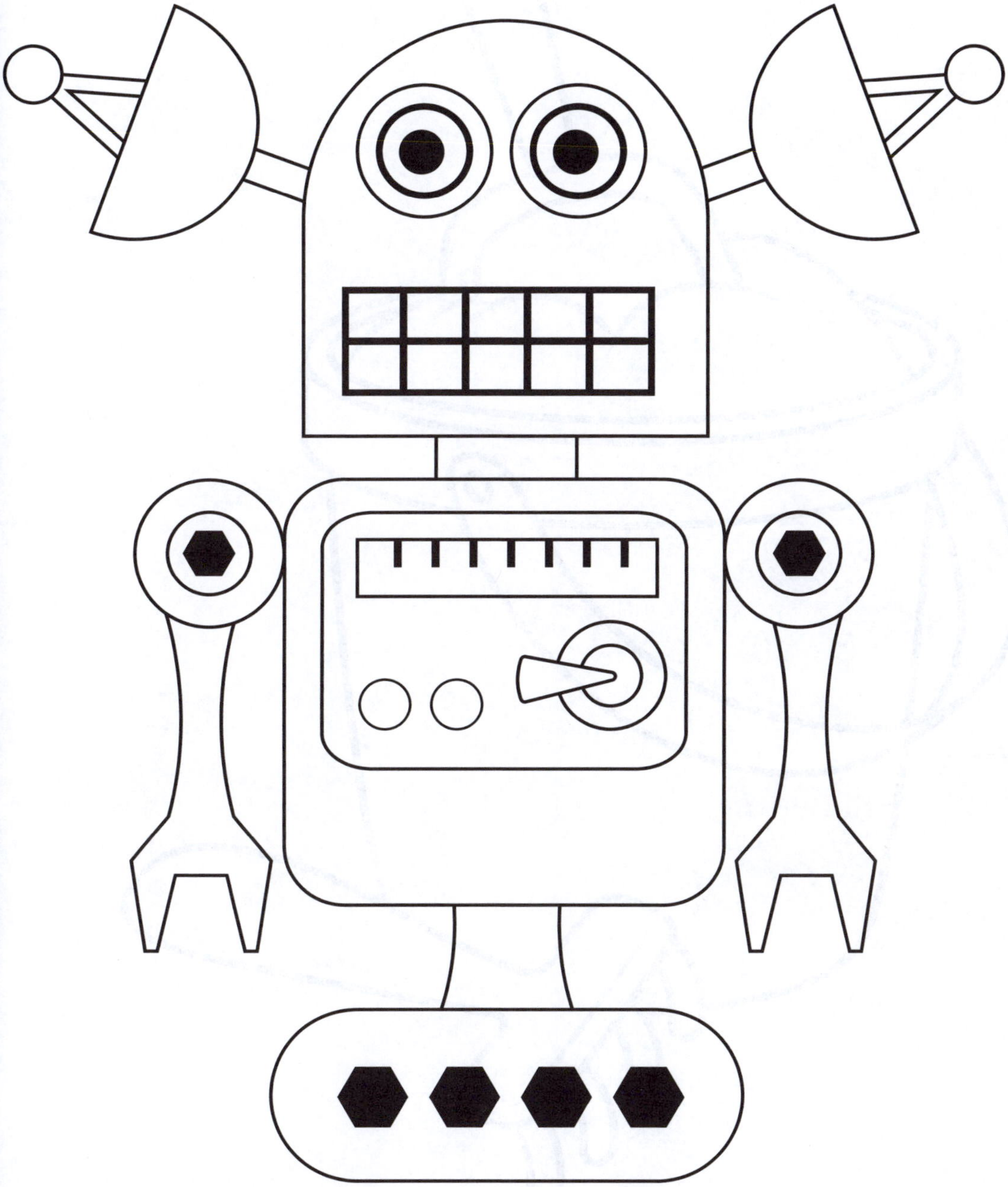

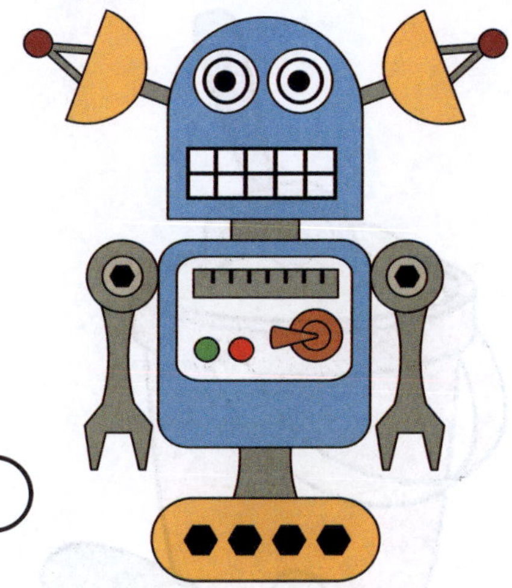

robot

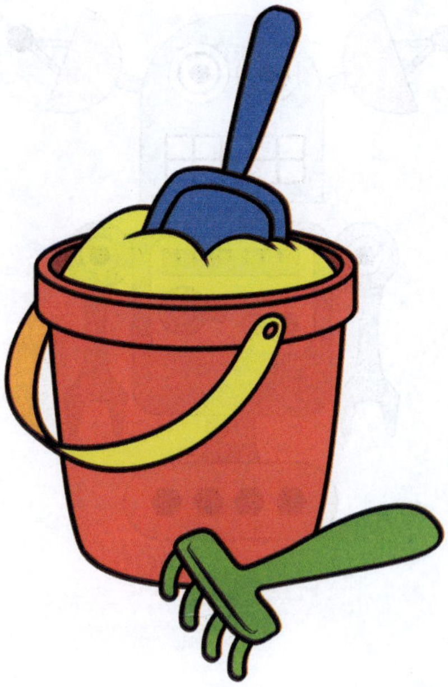

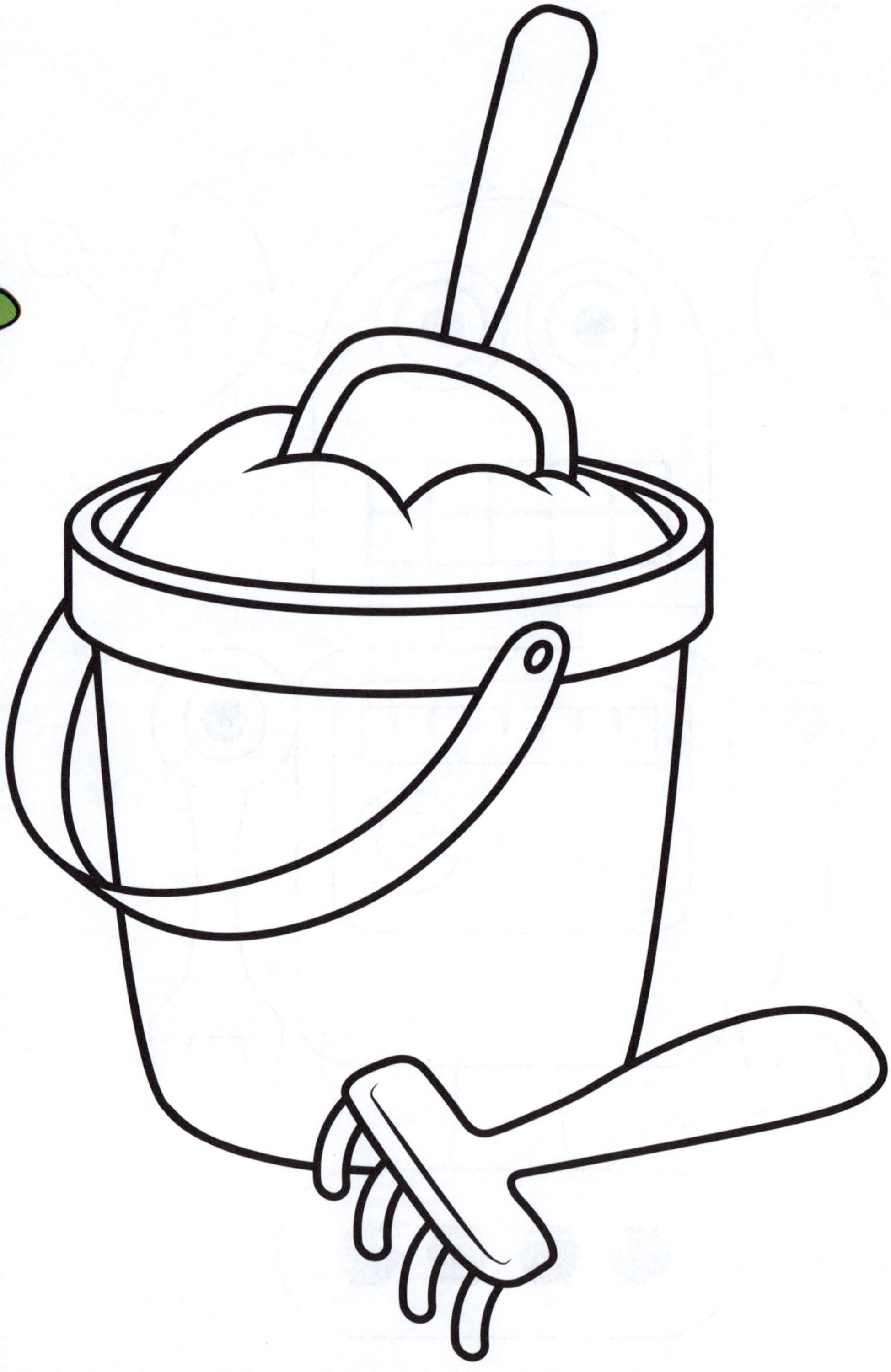

bucket and shovel

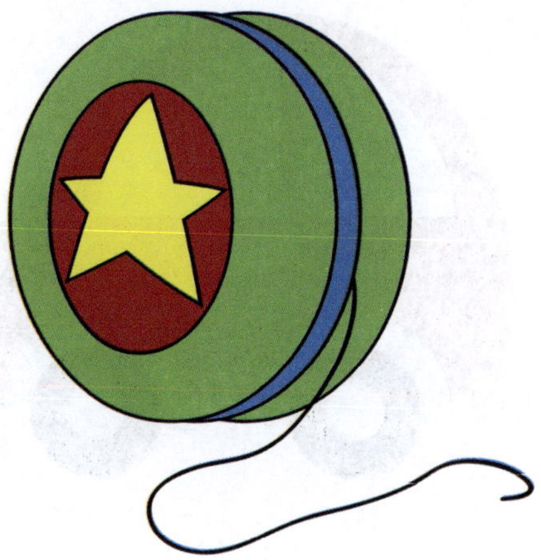

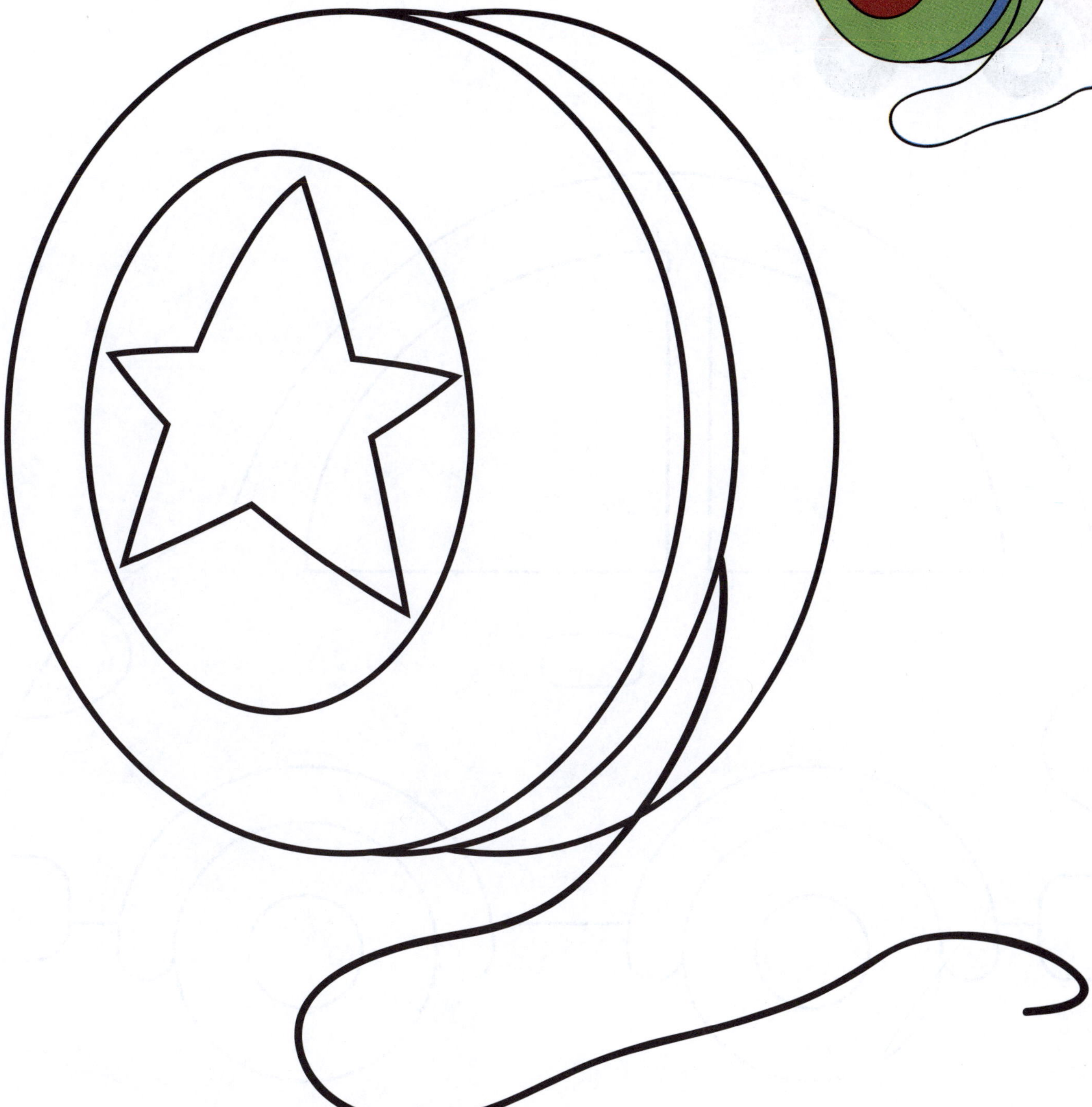

yo yo

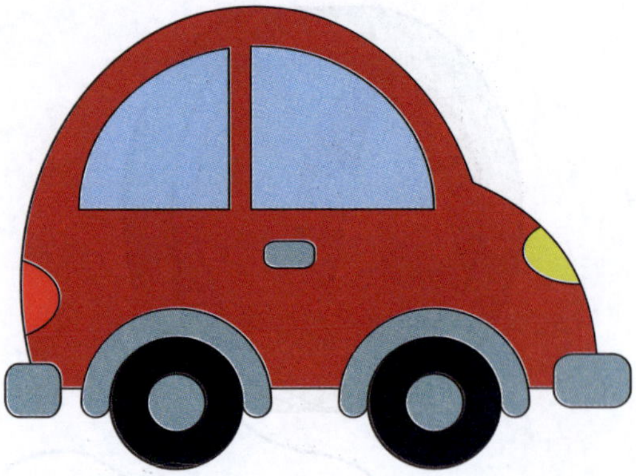

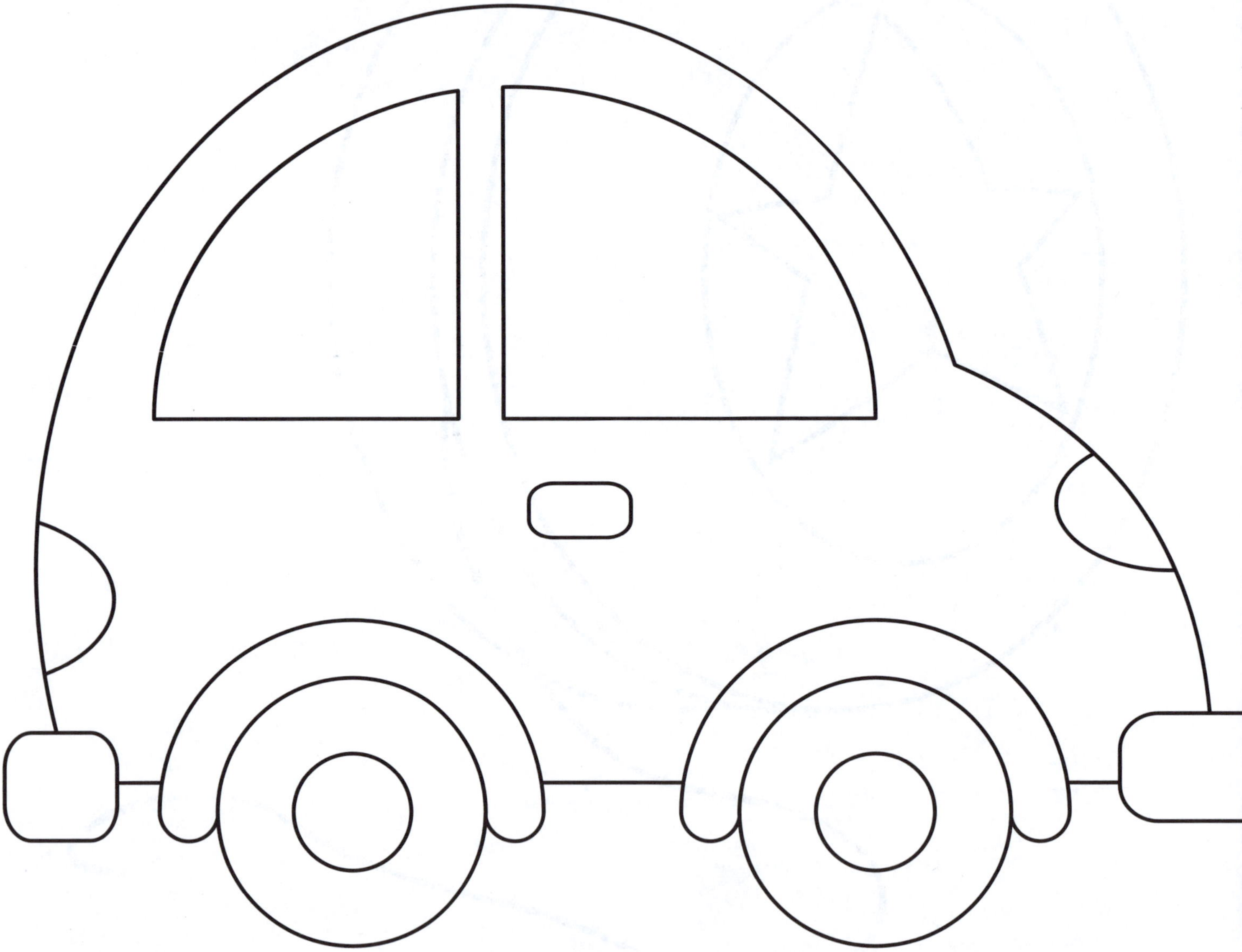

car

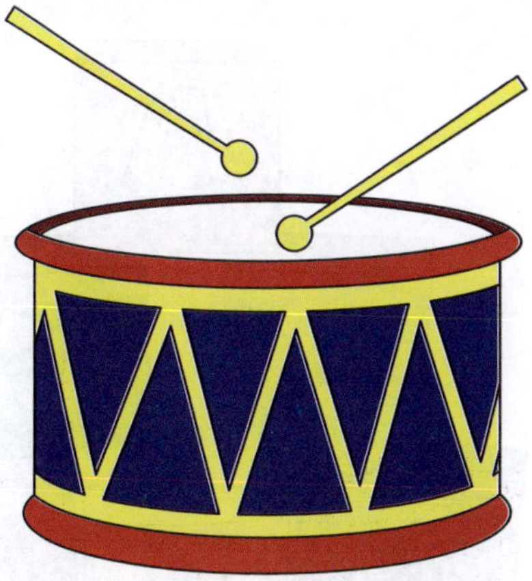

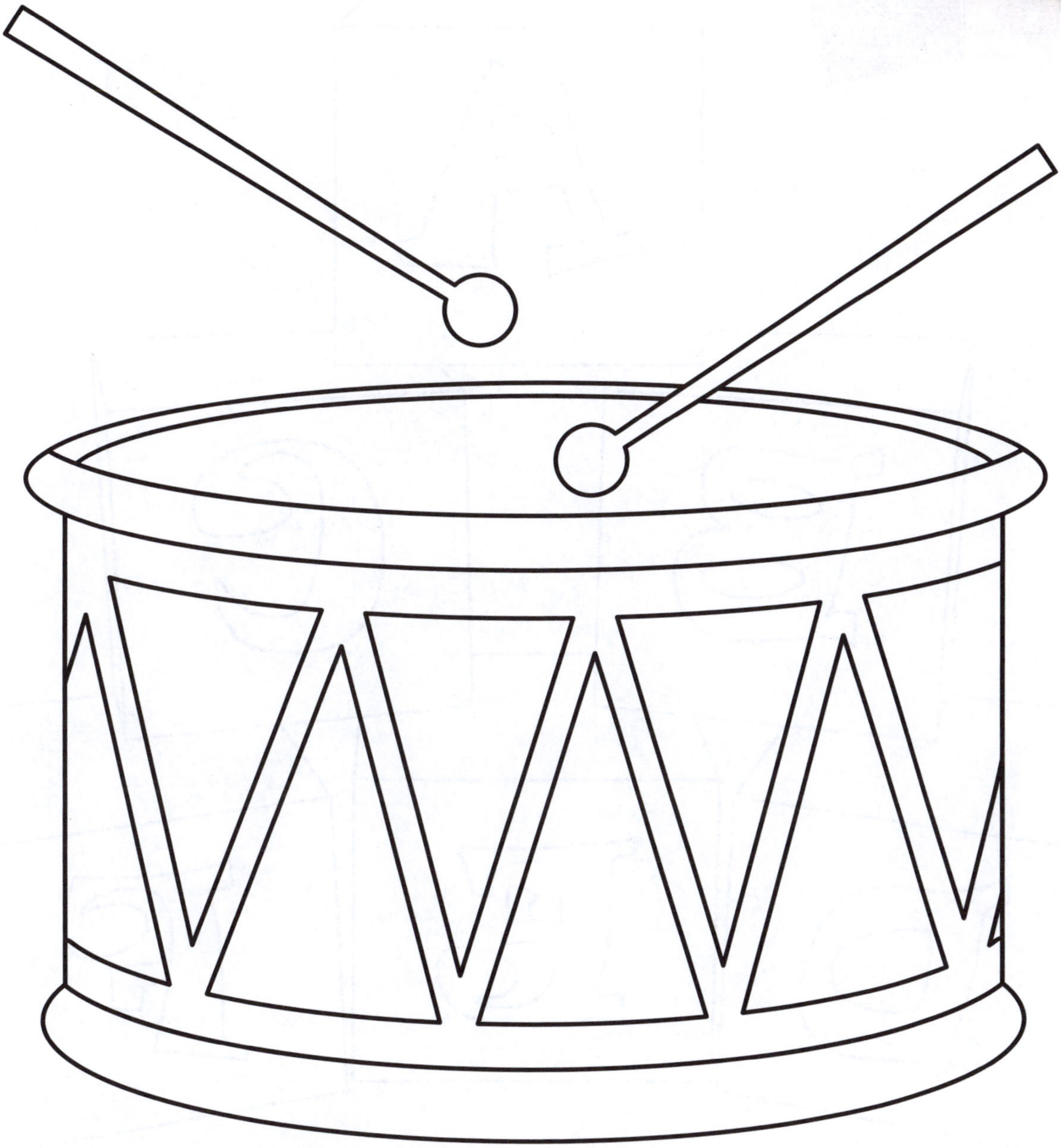

drum

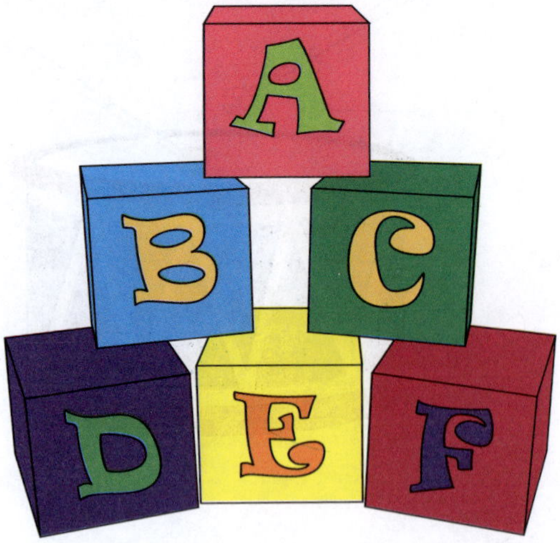

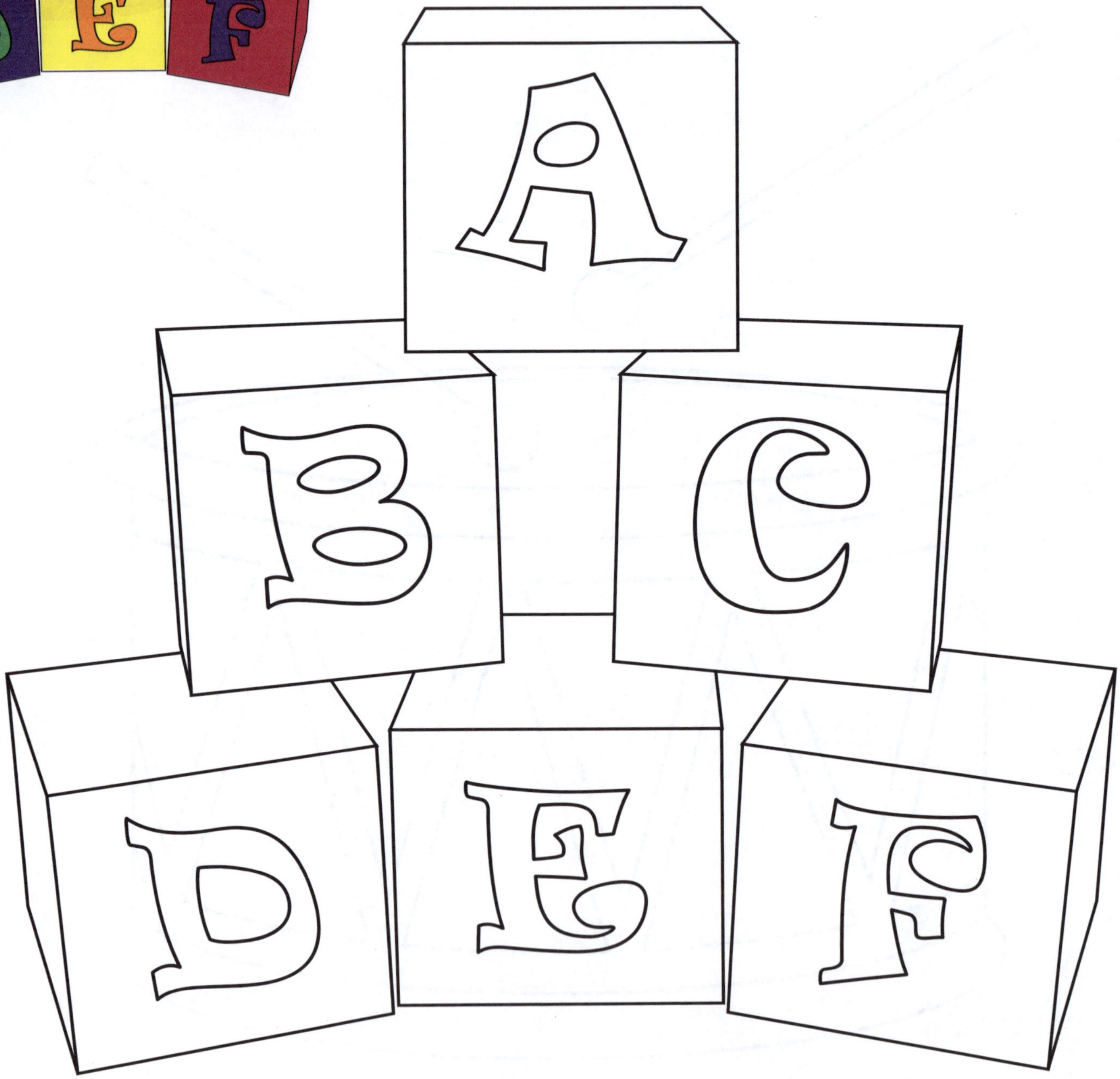

alphabet blocks